Chess Openings
for Kids

*Basic Insight into the Opening of
the Chess Game*

Table of Contents

Introduction 1

Chapter 1: What Is a Chess Opening? 3

Chapter 2: The Worth of Each Opening Piece 14

Chapter 3: Developing the Opening Characters 24

Chapter 4: The Top Basic Openings You Should
Know About 35

Chapter 5: Common Mistakes Made in the Opening
and How to Avoid Them 53

Chapter 6: Best Ways to Master the Opening Phase
in Chess 63

Quiz Answers 72

Conclusion 74

References 76

Introduction

Welcome, young enthusiasts, to your first steps into the world of chess. These are known as openings! Openings are the first few moves of any chess game. They are key to a good game, and a good start is a must-have advantage in any sport, and chess is not just any sport. It's a game of intellect and imagination, where every move matters and a mistake could mean your downfall. To play your best, you must know the best strategies and tactics and, in this book, you will take the first steps on your journey to mastering the art of the opening.

Just as artists carefully plan their masterpieces in advance, chess players carefully orchestrate their opening moves to set the stage for victory. Within these pages, you will learn how to make the best opening moves and how to take advantage of your opponent's mistakes. In this book, you will go on an adventure to discover the secrets of the opening phase of a chess game, which can ensure your victory early in the game.

In "Chess Openings for Kids," from the very first chapter, you will discover the true essence of chess openings, where creativity meets strategy, and why they are so significant.

Openings are usually intimidating to new players and may even be a weak point for seasoned players. As you progress, you'll gain valuable insights into the worth of each opening piece, understanding the strengths and weaknesses of your pieces. Correctly valuing your pieces enables you to make informed decisions during the opening and gives you a tactical edge over your opponents.

After that, you will know how to develop your opening pieces. Through careful guidance, you'll learn how to position your pieces strategically, maximize their potential, and set yourself up for a glorious checkmate.

In "Chess Openings for Kids," there's a curated selection of the top basic chess openings you should know. From the elegant Italian Game to the cheeky King's Gambit, you'll learn the advantages and disadvantages of the most famous chess openings in history. To truly master the opening phase, pay close attention to the range of effective techniques in this book. You'll discover the best ways to refine your skills with practice exercises, puzzles, and experienced advice. So, young chess enthusiasts, prepare to embark on this amazing quest. "Chess Openings for Kids" will empower you with the skills you need to start your chess journey on the right foot. Get ready to discover your strategic brilliance. The chessboard is waiting!

Chapter 1: What Is a Chess Opening?

Chess is a game of strategy and tactics. In it, you have to use your mind to outsmart or out-predict your opponent. A chess opening is the first few moves of the game, and it sets up the rest of the game. Learning about openings is an important part of honing your chess skills. Openings are set outlines you should follow to start the game on the right foot and be prepared for whatever your opponent does because, as in all sports, a good start makes a big difference in the outcome of the game. There are many different openings, each with its own unique advantages and disadvantages. So, in order to master an opening, you should know first what an opening is.

1. *Chess is a game requiring strategy and tactics. Source: https://pixabay.com/photos/chess-chessboard-board-game-3960184/*

The First Few Moves

Every chess game has three phases which are the opening, the middle game, and the endgame. The endgame generally has fewer pieces on the board, and at that stage, you may be searching for a checkmate or trying to promote a pawn to a queen. The middlegame has a lot of attacking and defending, and it involves trying to get into a better position against your opponent. The opening, which you're learning about in this book, is how the game begins. On average, the opening is the first ten moves of any game.

There are three key rules when controlling the center:

- Control the center
- Develop your pieces
- Protect your king

Control the Center

The chessboard consists of 64 squares. The center four squares are: d4, d5, e4, and e5. The files (the horizontal columns on the chessboard) of the kings and queens of both players meet on these squares. If you control them, you are in a good position moving forward because they allow for attacking your opponent's king and protecting yours.

These four squares are often called the Inner Center, the most central squares on the board. The ones surrounding them are known as the Outer Center. If you control them, you have a better position that allows you to protect and develop your pieces. The Outer Center consists of the following squares: c3, d3, e3, f3, f4, f5, f6, e6, d6, c6, c5, and c4.

But Why Is the Center So Important? Here's a soccer analogy to make this easier to understand. In soccer, there's a position called a midfielder, who starts the game in the middle of the field. They can attack, defend, and move freely on the field, which makes them very valuable for their team. In chess, controlling the center is as important as controlling it in soccer, and you can control and keep the center by doing two things. The first is that you actually put your pieces in the center, like playing pawn to e4, the most famous opening move in chess, for example. The second thing you can do, if you find playing for the center with your pieces right away too risky, is to aim your pieces at the center. If you're playing white, you can play your g-knight to f3 (Nf3), for example, which gives you control over the e5 and d4 squares. If you're playing black, you can play your b-knight to c6, which gives you control over the same two squares. This gives you a strategic advantage going forward because you 'protect' the pieces that you want to push to the inner center.

Developing Your Pieces

If you want to have a good position and an advantage over your opponent, you need to develop your pieces as quickly as possible. When you do that and control the center at the same time, you already have a great advantage over your opponent, even before the middlegame. Developing your pieces early, but not too early, allows them to have 'scope.' Scope represents the squares controlled by a piece. Developing your bishop, for example, to the center gives it a larger scope and control over a large number of squares across the chessboard. A large scope makes a piece more powerful and more useful.

In chess, you and your opponent each have an army of pieces so use it all. Some players make the mistake of moving one piece many times in the opening, which is not effective. Some players, for example, when playing white, start with the move g-knight to f3 (Nf3). Then, they move that same knight to e5, then to c4, then to e3. This is not effective because one piece by itself can't fight an entire army, even if it's the queen. If you're playing white and you want to start with the same move, Nf3, and you don't want to make this mistake, on your next move, move your other knight to c3 (Nc3), or you can push your pawn to e5 because the knight you first moved now protects it.

Let's imagine you're playing white, and your first move was pawn to e4. Your opponent responds with e5, attacking the center and blocking your e-pawn. On the second move, you play Nf3 attacking black's pawn on e5. Your opponent wants to defend their pawn, so they play Nc6. Now it's your turn. If you want to develop more pieces, you have two best moves: Nc3 and bishop to c4 (Bc4).

If you play Nc3, you defend your pawn on e4, and you attack the d5 square in case your opponent wants to push their pawn. This is a good move because it gives you more control over the center and defends your pieces, which are already there. If you play Bc4, you bring out an influential piece onto the Outer Center. This gives your bishop scope because it now controls the squares d5 and e6, and it threatens the pawn on f7. This move is good because it gives you an attacking advantage.

Protect Your King

2.   *The king is the most important chess piece. Source:*
https://pixabay.com/photos/chess-king-match-symbolism-
1226126/

The most important piece in chess is the king. Needless to say, you have to protect your king as best you can. Let's imagine you were given a pot of gold, and you were told to keep it safe from many people who were trying to take this gold away from you (your opponent's army of pieces). Would you put the gold in the middle of a room or in the corner inside a safe? In the middle of a room, it can be attacked from many different directions, and it is accessible to the other pieces, while if it is in the corner inside a safe, whoever wants to take the gold has to go to that corner and start unlocking the safe, which you can easily prevent by protecting the safe.

White's king starts on e1, and Black's king starts on e8, directly opposite to it on the other end of the same file. E1 and e8 are relatively close to the center, which you want to control and attack, and your opponent, in turn, wants to control and attack the center as well. The best thing to do to protect your king is to move it away from the center (the middle of the room) to a corner of the board (the safe in the corner). To achieve that, castling is your best option. The pieces that start on the corner of a chessboard are the rooks; the a1 and h1 rooks for white and a8 and h8 rooks for black. Castling is making your king and rook switch places so that the king is safer near the corner and the rook is closer to the center, where it can control squares and protect other pieces.

There are two ways to castle: Kingside and Queenside. Kingside castling (symbolized by 0-0) is when you castle your king with the rook on h1, which is when the rook is closer to the king, and Queenside castling (symbolized by 0-0-0) is when you castle your king with the rook on a1. Kingside castling is often the better choice because it leaves less space between the king and the edge of the board. So, if you castle Kingside with white, your king goes to g1, and your h-rook goes to f1. If you castle Queenside, with white too, your king goes to c1, and your a-rook goes to d1.

In Kingside castling, you leave one square empty next to the king, which is h1, while on the queen's side, you leave two squares empty, which are a1 and b1. Now, in order to castle, the king must 'see' the rook meaning there must be no pieces between the king and the rook you want to castle with. This is one of the reasons castling Kingside is a better option because you only need to develop your knight on g1 and your bishop on f1 in order to open the path for your king, while on the other side, you still have to develop your knight on b1, your bishop on c1, and the queen, which starts at d1.

Now, let's discuss what a Kingside 'castle' looks like. You have your king on g1 and your rook on f1, protecting the king from the left, and you have three pawns (the pawns on f1, g1, and h1) in front of the king, protecting it from your opponent's attacking pieces. If you move any of the pawns on f1, g1, or h1, you can still castle, but it's safer to castle before moving these pawns.

How to Castle

The earliest move you can castle on is the fourth move. This sounds hard, but it's actually very simple. Let's look at an example to illustrate this and make it easier. Imagine you're now playing a game and you're playing white, so you start. Your first move is e4, attacking the Inner Center right away, controlling key squares on the board, and attacking the d5 square. Your opponent responds with e5, going for the Inner Center as well and attacking the d4 square.

After that, you attack your opponent's pawn on e5 with the best move, Nf3. This way, with your knight, you're attacking your opponent's pawn, and you control the d4 square. Your opponent defends their pawn with Nc6 and attacks the d5 square as well. Now it's your turn. This is the third move. You play Bc4, developing your bishop, giving it scope, and controlling many squares on the board. Now your king can see your rook on h1, and the path between them is protected by the three pawns on f1, g1, and h1. Your opponent responds to your bishop move with Bc5, developing his own and giving it scope as well. Now's your fourth move. The best thing to do to protect your king now is to castle Kingside. So, you move your king to the g1 square and your h1-rook to f1. Now, you have great control over the center, you've developed a bishop and a knight, you've moved a pawn, and your king is safe in the corner of the board. From here on out, you can start strategizing better, and you can protect your king more easily.

Common Opening Mistakes

This chapter just discussed the basic principles of the best opening and how you can get a good start against your opponent. Now that you know what to do, let's teach you what not to do to avoid mistakes in the opening. You can even use these mistakes to your advantage if you want to.

So, the basic principles of the opening are controlling the center, developing pieces, and protecting the king. These are the best moves. Opening mistakes are simply doing the opposite of these three rules. Let's look at the first example.

Too Many Pawns

3.   Beginners often develop too many pawns. Source: https://pixabay.com/photos/special-independent-different-team-5012919/

Beginners often fall into the mistake of wanting to develop too many pawns. Advancing your army sounds like a good idea, but on the chessboard, it is important to protect your pieces and think strategically about every move, so moves like pawn to a4 or pawn to h4 are not the best in the opening, especially if your opponent is a good player.

Early Queen

The queen is the most powerful piece in chess and combines the powers of a rook and a bishop, and it is the piece with the most scope by default, which makes it a tempting piece to use. With the queen's powers, you can actually play a checkmate in four moves, known as the Scholar's Mate, which will be discussed later on. That said, you shouldn't develop your queen too early. Developing your pieces in the opening mainly refers to the knight and the bishop because they are 'minor' pieces that aren't as powerful as your queen and rooks, although they are influential and can be very useful in the middlegame and the endgame. The "Wayward Queen" attack is actually a famous opening that starts like this. White plays pawn to e4, Black plays e5, and then White plays queen to h5 (Qh5), developing the queen in the second move of the game. This makes the queen, your most valuable piece, very vulnerable and out in the open. Developing a knight or a bishop at the beginning is always a better choice.

King in the Center

This is when you violate the third principle of the opening, and you keep the king in the center. While it is not illegal to keep the king in the center, this is not your best choice because later on in the game, and maybe as early as the opening, you may have to develop many pieces and move many pawns. This leaves your king unprotected and your rooks away from each other, so castling as soon as possible is generally your best approach to protecting the king from the battle at the Inner and Outer Centers.

Castling is a crucial move in chess that accomplishes multiple objectives simultaneously. By castling, you protect the king by relocating it to a fortified position behind a wall of pawns. This maneuver shields your king from potential attacks, allowing you to focus more on attacking. Furthermore, it also facilitates the activation of your rooks. After castling, one of your rooks is activated, enabling it to come into play faster than it would if you didn't castle. If you empty your first rank after that, your rooks 'see' each other, which allows them to mutually defend each other and enables you to launch strong attacks while holding your defensive position.

Quiz

1) What are the three important goals of a chess opening?

A) Capturing pawns and attacking the opponent's king.

B) Controlling the center, developing pieces, and protecting the king.

C) Moving your pieces randomly, confusing your opponent, and hoping for the best.

2) What is a common mistake to avoid in the opening phase of a chess game?

A) Moving the same piece twice in a row.

B) Leaving your king unprotected.

C) Capturing your opponent's pieces without a plan.

3) You just started a game of chess, and you have the white pieces. You start with e4, and your opponent responds with e5. What is the best move for you right now?

A) Nf3, attacking the pawn on e5 and controlling the d4 square.

B) Nc3, attacking the d5 square and protecting the pawn on e4.

C) Qh5, developing your queen right away.

Chapter 2: The Worth of Each Opening Piece

Every chess game starts with a total of six different pieces on the board, which are pawns, knights, bishops, queens, rooks, and kings. Any piece can take any piece. However, because of their different potentials, not all pieces are equal.

Pawns move in one direction and are allowed only one or two moves ahead. They can take opposing pieces diagonally and can be easily blocked by any piece on the square right in front of them. Queens can move any number of squares diagonally, horizontally, and vertically, which makes them the strongest pieces on the chessboard. Due to this large difference in their abilities, pawns and queens have different 'values'. Knights, which move in an L-shape, bishops, which move any number of squares diagonally, and rooks, which move any number of squares horizontally or vertically, have different values as well.

Since chess is an unpredictable game of intellect and imagination, the value of any piece mostly depends on its current position on the board and the player using it, so no piece has a 'fixed' value. There are different systems for valuing a piece. However, the most famous values for chess pieces are the following:

A pawn, the weakest piece on the board, has the lowest value: one point. It can only move forward and capture opposing pieces one square away diagonally and to the front. **A knight**, which is the most elusive piece in chess, has the second lowest value: three points. The knight moves only in an L-shape, which limits its movement and makes it difficult to use.

Despite its limitations, a knight is the only piece that can jump over other pieces, and the right player knows how to utilize it to their advantage.

The bishop, which only moves diagonally, has the same value as a knight: three points. Each player starts with two bishops, one on a black square and another on a white square. But here's the trick. Bishops can only move to squares that are the same color they start on because diagonals on the board consist of squares of the same color. So, if a bishop starts on a dark square, it can only go to other dark squares.

4. *The bishop only moves diagonally. Source: MichaelMaggs, CC BY-SA 2.5 <https://creativecommons.org/licenses/by-sa/2.5>, via Wikimedia Commons: https://commons.wikimedia.org/wiki/File:Chess_piece_-_Black_bishop.JPG*

The bishop, like the knight, is not the strongest of pieces, but it can be very useful in the hands of the right player and can be very effective at blocking your opponent's moves and controlling a wide range of squares on the board. It is also a powerful character in the opening phase of the game because controlling more squares gives you a big advantage over your opponent.

The rook has a value of five points. Rooks are powerful pieces, and they are the trusty guards of the king. They can move any number of squares horizontally and vertically. They are very strong pieces in the endgame and effective in controlling space. Any chessboard is made up of squares lined up next to each other. The eight horizontal lines on a chessboard (rows) are called ranks, and the eight vertical lines (columns) are called files. In alphanumeric notation, the ranks (rows) are represented by numbers one through eight, and the files (columns) are represented by letters a through h. A single square represents an intersection between a file and a rank, and it is named accordingly, e4 and a1, for example.

Rooks are the best pieces in controlling ranks and files because you can move from one edge of the board to the other if you want to. An open file is basically a special road that only the rook can travel on. It's called 'open' because there are no other pieces blocking the rook's way. When you control an open file with your rook, it has the whole road to itself. This gives you a big advantage because you have more space to move your rook and attack your opponent's pieces and possibly their king.

During most endgames, players are down to their last pieces. You'll often see a player at the end of the game with only a king and a rook or a king and two rooks. During this phase, playing checkmate is a must, and the rook is the weakest piece that can do that when alone with the king. So, if you are down to your king and only one rook, you can still checkmate. You can't checkmate with your king and one knight, and you can't with your king and one bishop. This is one more thing that makes rooks a formidable and important piece on the chessboard.

Last but not least, **the queen**. The queen is the most powerful piece on the chessboard; it can move in any direction; diagonally, horizontally, and vertically. The queen is the most valuable piece, with a value of nine points! A queen's value is so high because it is useful in every position. The queen is the most intimidating piece on the board, as well, because it enables you to play the Scholar's Mate, which is checkmate in only four moves! However, the powers of the queen are only effective when used correctly. A queen, like a rook, can control an open file, and it can control diagonal space at the same time. A queen is a deadly piece in the hands of the right player in all phases of the game: opening, middlegame, and the endgame. The queen is, of course, capable of checkmate when alone with a king so if you are down to your king and one queen, you can still checkmate.

Position of a Piece

Pawns are the weakest pieces, and queens are the strongest pieces. Sometimes, however, the position of everything on the board changes the entire game. As you know, a pawn that gets to its opposing end of the board (the opposing back rank) gets to be promoted. You can promote your advanced pawn to a knight, a bishop, a rook, or even a queen. Most people, in most situations, of course, choose to promote to queen because of its power. Due to this, pawns, while weak at the beginning of the game, are very valuable in the middlegame and endgame because of their potential to become a queen. That said, the position of a game and the position of a piece in it determine its value in the game.

To illustrate that, imagine the following. You are playing with the black pieces. You have three pawns lined up in a diagonal formation. The first pawn is on the h7 square, the next one is on g6, and the last one is on f5. This special arrangement is called a pawn chain. This chain is especially useful because each pawn protects the one after it.

The pawn on h7 protects the pawn on g6. That one protects the pawn on f5. Moreover, the rook on g8 protects your h7 pawn, making all the pawns safe. In this case, the h7 pawn is called the base of the chain. It's a great way to keep your pawns safe and strong and to control important space on the board. This way, they are an effective team that works together and helps you on the road to victory. The chain controls space in two effective ways. First, they occupy squares, and they are protected, so no piece can take them. Second, they attack squares diagonally. The pawn on g6 controls the h5 square, and the f5 pawn controls the g4 and e4 squares.

Having a well-positioned pawn chain is great because it gives you offensive and defensive advantages against your opponent. You can extend the chain with another pawn or with another attacking piece because the chain protects it. So, in this scenario, your pawns, despite being the weakest pieces, have more value than before because they are in a good position.

Now, imagine playing with the white pieces, and at the beginning of the game, your opponent moves one of their pieces to the f3 square directly in front of your pawn on f2. Your pawn on f2 hasn't moved yet, so it feels a bit stuck, and it can't do anything to the enemy piece in front of it because pawns only take pieces that are one square in front of them diagonally. Here is where the excitement begins. You decide to use your clever thinking and take the attacking piece with another pawn, the pawn on e2, which starts right in front of the king. (Fun fact: the pawn on e2 is known as the King's Pawn because it is on the king's file and starts in front of the king). Now, you have a pawn on f2 (which hasn't moved) and a pawn on f3, which just moved to capture the attacking piece. These two pawns are now standing one in front of the other. This is known as a pawn stack. Here's the tricky part. Having a pawn stack is not a good position to be in. Here's why:

First of all, the pawn at the back can't protect the pawn at the front (unlike the pawn chain from the previous scenario) because if an opponent piece captures the front pawn, the back can't take the attacking piece. Secondly, in this way, the pawn at the front blocks the pawn at the back from moving forward. What's more, when you reach the endgame, it's harder to promote the pawn at the back because you have to move the one at the front first by pushing it to the opposing back rank, promoting it, and moving it away. Last but not least, in this particular scenario, the pawn you moved (which was on e2 before) used to block the king's file (the e-file). Now, the king is exposed to attacks from that file because there is no longer a pawn blocking the file. So, in this scenario, these two pawns are less valuable than before because they are in a bad position.

The same applies to all pieces in many different scenarios because of the unpredictability of a chess game. Remember that strategy and thinking ahead are very important in chess, and you must follow them from the beginning of the game in order to play a good opening and outsmart your opponent in all phases of the game.

Game Situation

Now you understand the values of chess pieces, and you've looked at scenarios where you have to be careful about your position. If you found any of this confusing, don't worry! The whole point is that the situation of the game is what decides the real value of a piece. The points mentioned before are just statistical value that doesn't apply in every situation. You could have more valuable pieces on the board than your opponent, and at the same time, your opponent could be one move away from checkmating you. These dangerous situations often call for what's called a trade. A trade is when you exchange pieces of equal statistical value with your opponent.

Imagine you are playing with the white pieces. You play the first move. E4. Your opponent replies with e5. On the second move, you play Nf3, attacking the pawn on e5. Shockingly, your opponent replies with pawn to d5, attacking your pawn on e4 instead of defending their pawn on e5. So, you decide to take the pawn on e5 with your knight (Nxe5). Then, your opponent takes your pawn on e4 with their pawn, which was on d5. This way, you took one pawn, and your opponent took one pawn. This is an equal trade, which reduces the amount of material on the board. In chess, simplification is almost always best, and trades are a good way to simplify a chess game because you don't lose your position, and you allow for more movement on the board. So, if you're ever in a pinch, try exchanging (trading) pieces with your opponent and you may just avoid a checkmate!

Trading pieces with your opponent means you each capture a piece or pieces of equal value. In the points system, one pawn is worth one point, and one bishop is worth three, so technically, a bishop is worth three pawns. Losing a piece doesn't always mean you're 'losing.' Imagine you're in the endgame, and you have one queen and two rooks, and your opponent has one queen and one rook or no rooks. In this case, trading queens gives you the advantage because you can use your two rooks since your opponent doesn't have a queen to counter them. This shows the beauty of simplification.

Always remember that even though chess depends on prediction, it is one of the most unpredictable games ever. So, the real value of a piece isn't set in stone and depends on how you use it. The points mentioned before are just numbers that don't always apply. So, embrace the fluidity and dynamic nature of the game and know that it requires creativity and the ability to adapt to the different situations you encounter. Instead of thinking about rules, think about how you can control the game and outplay your opponent.

Remember that a good start to your game, your skill, and intellect coupled with exquisite strategy and finesse are things that help you toward victory rather than having the strongest pieces. The opening, in fact, plays a part in "setting the values" of pieces for the rest of the game, which will be discussed in the next chapter.

Quiz

1) Which piece is considered the most powerful in the game?

   A) The Bishop

   B) The Queen

   C) The Rook

2) Pawns arranged diagonally are called a:

   A) Pawn chain

   B) Pawn stack

   C) File

3) True or False: The value of a chess piece can change depending on the position and stage of the game.

   A) True

   B) False

Chapter 3: Developing the Opening Characters

Protecting your pieces is crucial because their value can change as the game progresses. For example, rooks become incredibly valuable during the Endgame, so try not to lose a rook before then unless you have to. The same applies to a queen. As the most powerful piece, it is incredibly useful throughout the entire game, especially the endgame. However, despite the queen's unmatched powers, you should develop it a bit later than other pieces like the bishop, because the pieces you develop early are more likely to be traded and are more exposed to danger.

Each piece has a unique role to play. The pawns, like brave foot soldiers, step forward to control the center. Knights, with their fancy horse-like moves, leap into action to protect their allies. Bishops, resembling wise advisors, carefully position themselves to control space and help their fellow pieces on the way to victory. Rooks patiently await their grand entrance into the endgame.

The Danger of Early Development

There is a famous chess opening called the Wayward Queen Attack. This starts with white playing pawn to e4. Black responds with pawn to e5. Now, both players have pawns in the inner center and are attacking central squares. This looks like a good position until white plays something interesting: moving their queen to h5 (Qh5). Before going into the rest of the opening, let's think about this position for a minute.

White has one pawn in the inner center on e4, which attacks the d5 square and blocks Black's pawn on e5 from advancing. Black has one pawn in the inner center as well on e5, which attacks the d4 square and blocks White's pawn on e4 from advancing, and White has their queen on h5, which attacks Black's pawn on e5. At first, this seems like a good position for White, but Black has many options to make things difficult for them.

First of all, Black can now develop pieces like their bishops and their knights to protect their pawn on e5. Furthermore, they can play a move that 'kicks' the queen away. Kicking in chess is when you push a developed piece away from your pieces and back toward its own army. Black also has the chance to directly attack White's queen. The best move for Black in this situation is Nc6, which defends the pawn on e5. This way, if White takes the pawn on e5 with their queen, the knight on c6 easily captures the queen. Now, white can't take the pawn on e5 without losing their queen. But White still wants to play checkmate, so they play their white bishop to c4 (Bc4), attacking the f7 square on Black's side. At the moment, the f7 square is a weak spot in Black's lines because it is directly next to the king, and White is attacking it with two pieces: the queen from h5 and the bishop from c4.

This way, White is one move away from checkmate, and they think they're winning. However, Black has the clever move, pawn to g6, directly attacking White's queen, which has no defenders. The queen can't take the attacking pawn because it'll be taken by one of Black's pawns, so the queen has no choice but to move back, and White's attack fails.

Overall, the Wayward Queen Attack might seem powerful, but it's actually a risky opening and can be easily defended against. This teaches you to choose your opening moves wisely, as the queen, despite its amazing powers, is not a good piece to start with.

5. Developing your pieces too early can be risky. Source:
https://pixabay.com/photos/strategy-chess-board-game-1080527/

Learning from the Defense

Let's take a quick look at how Black defended against White's Wayward Queen Attack in this last example. First, they developed their knight, which is an excellent choice that defends the vulnerable pawn on e5 and attacks the center as well. Now, Black's developed knight defends the pawn and controls the d4 square in the inner center. After White's bishop moved to c4, Black cleverly moved their pawn to g6, which attacked the queen. Pushing a pawn seems like a simple move, but at this time, it is the move because it attacks the opponent's queen. In this way, Black has moved the right pieces to their right places at the right time.

When White's queen falls back and has to quit its early assault on Black's king, Black now has a good starting position to continue their game and further develop pieces in the opening, while White has to get their pieces to safety and move the queen (which is out in the open) out of the danger of Black's attack. Now, apply what you've learned.

What to Develop

In the first chapter, you learned about the three main principles of an opening:

- Controlling the center

- Developing your pieces

- Protecting your king

Believe it or not, you can do all three at the same time. Each of these principles serves a crucial purpose in the initial phases of the game, and they are not isolated concepts but rather interdependent strategies that support one another. You can develop your pieces in order to control the center and allow for castling, which protects your king.

When you aim to control the center, you're essentially asserting dominance over the most influential squares on the board. The center holds the key to both mobility and control.

This concept isn't isolated from the others; it lays the foundation for the development of your pieces and the safety of your king. As you place your pieces strategically to exert control over the center, you're not just vying for space but also setting the stage for your upcoming maneuvers.

Let's say you have the white pieces. First, think about what you want to do. Chess is the ultimate game of strategy, so come up with a strategy that you want to follow.

The key is not to think too far ahead. Don't start thinking about the endgame before making the first move. Focus on the opening. The opening is what 'opens' the game, so to speak, and sets everything into motion. Remember what you've learned. The first thing to do is to control the center. Keep that in mind and start the game.

Before you make your first move, take a look at your pieces for a moment. What can you move? Only your pawns and your two knights. Now, if you want to control the center, think about this. Which piece can control the center best? Pawn or knight? If you move a knight, it'll attack two squares in the center, sure, but it's not 'on' the center. It can't reach the center right away and has to wait for the next move. Your pawns, on the other hand, can get there right away. You have two pawns that can go to the inner center: your pawns on e2 and d2 (the King's Pawn and the Queen's Pawn, respectively). Take it easy and choose the classic move pawn to e4. Now, you have a pawn in the center. This is a good start. Your opponent is an experienced player, so they play pawn to e5, attacking the center just like you.

It's your turn again. Take a look at your pieces again. What can you move? You can still move your knights, and now you can move two more pieces; the queen and the white-squared bishop, which start on d1 and f1, respectively.

The bishop is a good opening piece, but it's not very useful at the moment because e5 is a dark square, so the white-squared bishop can't attack your opponent's pawn on e5, which is controlling part of the center. Your best choice here is to develop your knight that starts on g1. You play Nf3 attacking the pawn on e5. Good job! You're attacking the center.

Your opponent has played Nc3 defending their pawn. Now, you can't take the pawn on e5 because if you capture it, your opponent will capture your knight, which is a more valuable piece (at the moment). For the next move, to gain a better position, you have two options. The first one is to develop your other knight or to develop your white-squared bishop, and both moves are good.

Your first option is to move your other knight to c3 (Nc3). This gives you more access to the inner center. Your first knight (the one on f3) attacks e5 and d4. If you make the move Nc3, you control d5, and you defend your pawn on e4. Great move! You now have eyes on the whole inner center, and you're prepared to develop more pieces. Your opponent can't play pawn to d5 now because, remember, you control that square. From here on, you can develop your pieces comfortably because you mostly control the center, and you have gained enough space to move freely.

Your second option is bishop to c4 (Bc4). First, your bishop gains scope and controls a vast amount of space. What's more, it attacks the pawn on f7, which is right next to your opponent's king. This could mean trouble for your opponent if you follow up correctly. Also, you back up your pawn on e4 in assaulting the center; you have two pieces attacking the d5 square, so the opponent can't advance their pieces comfortably. Last but not least, you can castle on your next move! Your king can now see your rook, and you have the three pawns on f2, g2, and h2 lined up to protect your castle. You're one step closer to moving your king away from the center and to safety. Here's the tricky part. Both moves are good, so which one should you choose?

When to Develop

Your choice here depends on your strategy. If you want to play a slower game and develop your pieces comfortably, Nc3 is the move for you. This way, you have your eyes on the center, and you're preparing to develop your other pieces along with your two knights, who have now both left their starting squares. This move gives you a good defensive position and chances to further develop your pieces. With this move, you've initiated a world-famous chess opening called the Three Knights Game.

On the other hand, if you want a more dynamic and quicker game, you should play Bc4. First of all, it allows you to move your king to safety by castling on the next move. After that, you can start your attack on your opponent's king, and you can develop your other knight and then the rest of your pieces to pave your road to victory. Remember the f7 square, too. The f7 square is right next to Black's King. Moving your bishop to c4 gives you an offensive advantage later on because you attack a vulnerable square that's close to your opponent's king. It is also the move that gives you control over more space. If you play it, you initiate an opening called the Italian Game, which is arguably the most famous opening in all of chess.

Quiz

1) You're playing with the white pieces. You start with e4, and your opponent plays e5. Then, you play Nf3, and your opponent responds with Nc6. Which move, in this case, starts the Three Knights Game?

   A) Bishop to c4 (Bc4)

   B) Knight to c3 (Nc3)

   C) Queen to e2 (Qe2)

2) Which piece is the best to control the most space early on in the game?

   A) Queen

   B) Knight

   C) Bishop

3) Which piece should you avoid developing too early in the opening?

   A) Rook

   B) Knight

   C) Queen

4) In the context of the opening moves, what is the significance of controlling the center in chess?

   A) It helps protect the king from early attacks.

   B) It allows for easier pawn promotions.

   C) It provides a strong position for launching an endgame strategy.

   D) It influences the mobility and control of the board.

5) Which move can Black make to counter the Wayward Queen Attack and force White's queen to retreat?

   A) Pawn to g6

   B) Knight to c6

   C) Pawn to e4

   D) Bishop to c4

6) What is the Italian Game in chess, and what does it involve?

   A) An opening that involves sacrificing the queen for an attack.

   B) A strategy where all pieces are developed in the center simultaneously.

   C) A famous opening initiated by moving the knight to f3.

   D) A tactic where the queen is used to control the center squares.

7) Which piece becomes incredibly valuable during the endgame, and players are advised not to lose it before that point?

   A) Pawn

   B) Knight

   C) Rook

   D) Bishop

8) Why should players be cautious about developing their queen too early in the game?

   A) The queen is weak in the opening phase.

B) The queen's power is unmatched, but it's susceptible to danger.

C) Developing the queen early increases the chance of a stalemate.

D) The queen can't move until other pieces are developed.

9) What is the term used in chess to describe when a developed piece is pushed away from its own army and back toward the opponent's pieces?

A) Retreat

B) Skewer

C) Kicking

D) Sacrifice

10) In the Wayward Queen Attack, why is Black able to defend against White's early assault on the king's side?

A) Black advances their central pawns aggressively.

B) Black develops their bishops and knights to protect their pawns.

C) Black plays a move that threatens White's queen.

D) Black sacrifices their queen to counter White's strategy.

11) What are the three main principles of an opening in chess, as mentioned in the text?

A) Protecting the queen, controlling the center, and promoting pawns.

B) Attacking the opponent's king, trading pieces, and castling.

C) Developing the rooks, controlling the opponent's pieces, and sacrificing pawns.

D) Controlling the center, developing your pieces, and protecting your king.

Chapter 4: The Top Basic Openings You Should Know About

Studying basic openings gives you an edge against your opponent. In this chapter, you'll come across some of the most famous openings in the history of chess. Each one has many variations, advantages, and disadvantages for both players. Along with variations, there are also many types of chess openings. In this chapter, you'll learn three openings of the following types; Open game and Gambit. The first two are open game openings, and the third one is a gambit. Note that gambit openings are more advanced.

Get a chessboard in front of you to replicate the openings and visualize the moves.

The Italian Game

The Italian Game is one of the oldest chess openings, dating back to the 1500s. To play it, White starts with e4, attacking the center as usual. Black responds with the classic e5. The second move starts, and white plays Nf3 attacking Black's pawn on e5. Black defends their pawn by moving their knight to Nc6. Then, White plays the move bishop to c4 Bc4, completing the Italian Game. This opening is written in short form in the following format:

1. e4 e5
2. Nf3 Nc6
3. Bc4

This format is very simple. Each row represents a move and its order. The first row is the first move, the second row is the second move, and so on. Each move is divided into two parts, and since White always starts, the first part of every move is White's move, and the second part is Black's move. So, as you see in the first row, e4 is White's first move, and e5 is Black's first move. This row, as a whole, represents the first move. You can look at this format as columns, as well. The first column on the left is White's moves, and the column beside it is Black's moves.

Now, let's talk about the Italian Game. The Italian is a simple opening, and the development of pieces seems basic, so some players consider it inferior. However, it has the potential to transform into very exciting middlegames that lead to even more exciting endgames.

The Italian starts simple and without trouble, so it is useful if you don't know how to start. This is renowned for its simplicity, and it serves as the ideal choice for those seeking an easy starting point. It proves particularly beneficial if you're unsure of how to start. There are three variations of the Italian Game that follow the moves you saw above. These three variations all depend on Black's third move, which is the missing move in the description above. These variations hold immense significance, as they reveal diverse strategic possibilities based on the choices made by Black at this critical point in the game.

The Giuoco Piano

If Black plays Bc5, the game looks like this:

1. e4 e5

2. Nf3 Nc6

3. Bc4 Bc5

6. *The Giuoco Piano variation. Source: Hfjhjoüjklij4, CC BY-SA 4.0 <https://creativecommons.org/licenses/by-sa/4.0>, via Wikimedia Commons: https://commons.wikimedia.org/wiki/File:Italian_Game.jpg*

This is called the Giuoco Piano variation. This is the variation in which Black copies White's bishop development and strikes at the center just like Black. In this way, both players are in an attacking position, and they are both ready to castle Kingside on the next move. Naturally, White's next move is usually castling Kingside (represented by the symbol 0-0), and Black does the same. If you're playing either Black or White, this opening gives you the chance to play aggressively and allows you to defend and attack at the same time. Practice it well and see how your games go. The Italian, thanks to how simple it is, is a great opening to practice and master.

Note that the Giuoco Piano shifts the focus to piece development and control of the center. The seemingly boring copy-cat move sequence gives both sides equal control of the center. Now, both have had a good start, and it's up to the better player to try and gain the upper hand.

The Evans Gambit

The Evans Gambit is an extension of the Giuoco Piano where White, on the third move, moves their pawn on b2 to b4.

1. e4 e5
2. Nf3 Nc6
3. Bc4 Bc5
4. b4

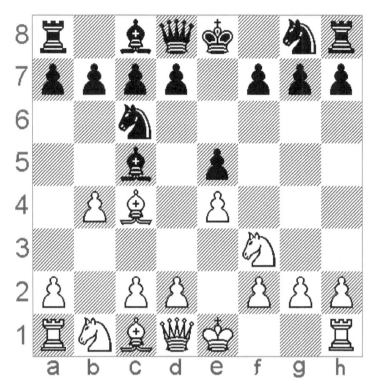

7. *The Evans Gambit. Source: No machine-readable author provided. Fenya~commonswiki assumed (based on copyright claims)., CC BY-SA 3.0 <http://creativecommons.org/licenses/by-sa/3.0/>, via Wikimedia Commons: https://commons.wikimedia.org/wiki/File:Evans_gambit.png*

The new pawn White just pushed is undefended. Thus, White is 'sacrificing' their pawn. If Black takes the pawn with their bishop, they've accepted the Gambit. If they don't and they move their bishop away from danger, they've refused the Gambit. This move seems simple but allows White to play more aggressively later on, and games that start like this usually involve more attacking and tactical moves.

The Two Knights Defense

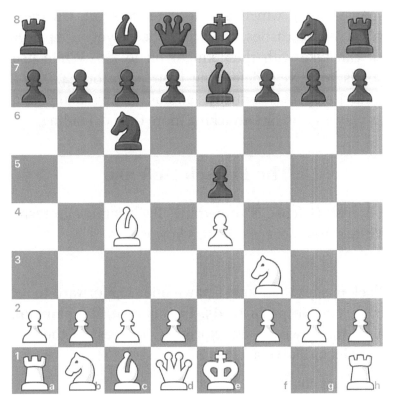

8. *The Two Knights Defense. Source: Hfjhjoiijklij4, CC BY-SA 4.0 <https://creativecommons.org/licenses/by-sa/4.0>, via Wikimedia Commons: https://commons.wikimedia.org/wiki/File:Hungarian_Defense_of _the_Italian_Game.jpg*

This is the third variation of the Italian Game, and it goes like this:

1. e4 e5

2. Nf3 Nc6

3. Bc4 Nf6

In this variation, Black plays the smarter move. Copying White's move and playing Bc5 like the Giuoco Piano is easy, but it's not advantageous to Black. Black now has control over most of the center, and the new knight is now attacking the pawn on e5, which has no defenders yet. On the next move, if White castles, they lose the pawn on e4 because Black can take with their knight on f6. So, White usually responds with Nc3, defending their pawn on e4. The Two Knights Defense is actually famous among many famous chess players who like attacking more than defending.

The French Defense

The French Defense is something Black can use in response to White's first move, e4. Here's how it goes:

1. e4 e6

Black pushes their king's pawn one step forward to set up their next move pawn to d5. In this case, the pawn on e6 defends the pawn on d5. Normally, the rest of the French Defense looks like this:

1. e4 e6
2. d4 d5

9. The French Defense. Source: Acagastya, CC0, via Wikimedia Commons: https://commons.wikimedia.org/wiki/File:French_Defence.png

This is called the mainline variation, where White sees an opportunity to take one more square in the inner center, so they play pawn to d4. Now, White might think they have good control over the center, but then, Black attacks White's pawn on e4 with the move pawn to d5. Now, Black has a little pawn chain! The base of the chain is the pawn on e6, and the top of the chain is the pawn on d5. Black now has a strong defensive position and a strong attacking position because they are attacking the pawn on e4 and, in turn, the inner center.

One of the strongest advantages of the French Defense is that it can evolve into various pawn structures that help you win the game, which allows you to adopt different plans and tactics to gain an advantage. Also, when you play the French, remember that you still have knights; you can and should move them. Here are some of the most common variations of the French Defense.

The Exchange Variation

In this variation, the game goes like this:

1. e4 e6

2. d4 d5

3. exd5 (White captures Black's pawn on d5 with their pawn on e4. Black captures back by taking White's pawn with their pawn on e6)

10. The Exchange Variation. Source: Hffhjoiijklij4, CC BY-SA 4.0 <https://creativecommons.org/licenses/by-sa/4.0>, via Wikimedia Commons: https://commons.wikimedia.org/wiki/File:Exchange_Variation_of _the_French_Defense.jpg

In this exchange (or trade), both sides lose one pawn, but it's fair because they're of equal value. The board looks symmetrical, with each player having one pawn in the center; White has a pawn on d4, and Black has one on d5. The kings also face each other on an open file. Even though it looks balanced, Black still has an advantage because they have better attack opportunities and can control more of the board.

The Advance Variation

This is a more interesting variation of the French Defense, and it goes like this:

1. e4 e6

2. d4 d5

3. e5

11. *The Advance Variation. Source: Hfjhjoiijklij4, CC BY-SA 4.0 <https://creativecommons.org/licenses/by-sa/4.0>, via Wikimedia Commons: Hfjhjoiijklij4, CC BY-SA 4.0 <https://creativecommons.org/licenses/by-sa/4.0>, via Wikimedia Commons*

White chooses to escape the attacking pawn by taking a step forward. Now, White has a pawn past the center. Black's defenses are now disrupted: White has a pawn past the center. Black's pawns on d5 and e6 are blocked by White's pawns on d4 and e5, respectively, limiting their movement. An interesting continuation of this variation happens if Black's third move is Nc6.

1. e4 e6

2. d4 d5

3. e5 Nc6

Black is now attacking both White's pawns at the same time! This applies great pressure on White's attack and puts White at a disadvantage.

The Tarrasch Variation

This is one of the more interesting variations of the French Defense, and it goes like this:

1. e4 e6

2. d4 d5

3. Nd2

12. *The Tarrasch Variation. Source: Hfjhjoiijklij4, CC BY-SA 4.0 <https://creativecommons.org/licenses/by-sa/4.0>, via Wikimedia Commons: https://commons.wikimedia.org/wiki/File:Tarrasch_Variation_of _the_French_Defense.jpg*

As usual, Black is attacking White's pawn on e4 with the pawn on d5. White responds cleverly by moving their knight to d2, right in front of the queen. The knight on d2 is now defending the pawn on e4! Now, if Black captures the pawn on e4, they lose a pawn themselves, and it's another trade, but White's knight becomes more developed and is present in the inner center, threatening Black's defenses. Despite White's clever move, Black is still at an advantage because they can play the move Nf6, which puts more pressure on the e4-pawn. This variation is great for Black because it gives them fantastic attacking opportunities while maintaining a solid defense around their pieces and their king. So, the better option for White is defending their pawn on e4 with their other knight by playing Nc3, which is called the mainline variation.

The French Defense is one of the most popular openings ever because it is very strong and reliable with many advantages for Black. When Black plays the French Defense, they create a solid defensive and offensive setup right from the beginning of the game. They build a fortress around their pieces and prepare to launch powerful attacks on the center and on their opponent's king. It also offers Black flexibility because most of its variations allow them to have the upper hand against White. The possible variations allow Black to play confidently because of the control they provide over the board.

The Queen's Gambit

All the examples discussed so far start with White playing e4. While e4 is a reliable opening move that attacks the center directly, you don't always have to play it. If you still want to control the inner center and attack it right away, you have another option: d4. The pawn which starts on d2 is called the queen's pawn because it starts on the square right in front of the queen. Starting with the move, d4 has many advantages. The first is that your king is safer than usual because if you play e4, your king is exposed right away, and your opponent can develop some deadly attacks. The second advantage is that it helps you develop your queen better and focus more on your Queenside pieces, which are the bishop on c1, the knight on b1, and the rook on a1 if you're playing white. Keep in mind that this opening is a little advanced compared to the Italian and French, so don't worry if it looks harder to follow than the other two. Don't let that deter you from playing it and learning from it.

So, take a look at a world-famous opening that starts with d4, and that is the Queen's Gambit.

The Queen's Gambit starts very simple:

1. d4 d5

2. c4

Instead of the usual e4 e5, the game starts on the queen's file (the d-file). White plays d4, and Black responds with d5. Both players are now attacking the center, and the game looks normal until White plays the move pawn to c4. Black just offered a free pawn to White. This seems like an odd move at first, but this is the Queen's Gambit. White is offering a pawn to Black, and Black chooses to accept the Gambit by taking the pawn or refuse it by not taking it.

The Queen's Gambit Accepted

1. d4 d5
2. c4 dxc4

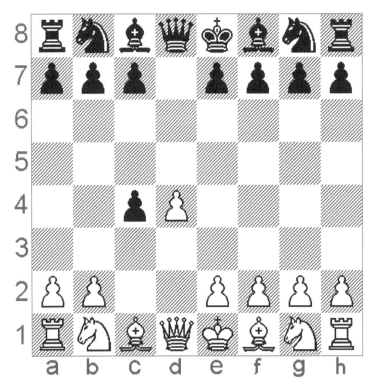

13. *Queen's Gambit Accepted. Source: No machine-readable author provided. Fenya~commonswiki assumed (based on copyright claims)., CC BY-SA 3.0 <http://creativecommons.org/licenses/by-sa/3.0/>, via Wikimedia Commons: https://commons.wikimedia.org/wiki/File:Queens_Gambit_accept ed.png*

From then on, White usually plays e4. White has two pawns in the inner center (on d4 and e4), and White's white bishop on f1 is attacking Black's pawn on c4. Black is now in trouble; they have no pieces in the inner center, and their only advanced pawn is under attack. This is the first variation of the Queen's Gambit, where Black accepts the gambit by taking the pawn.

Black can defend against the bishop's attack by moving their pawn on b7 to b5 or by moving their white bishop to e3.

In both cases, Black's c4 pawn has a fellow piece defending it; however, White is in a much better position. White has control over the center and can attack Black in many ways. This is the most common variation, mainly because it's easier to play, so give it a try and see how your game goes.

The Queen's Gambit Declined

The Queen's Gambit can be a very effective trap against many players, even when it's declined. The declined variation goes like this:

1. d4 d5

2. c4 c6

3. Nc3 Nf6

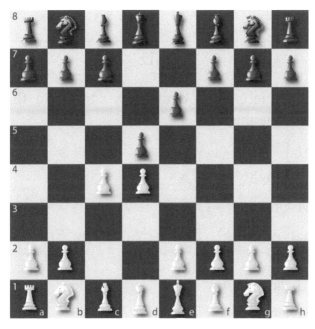

14. Queen's Gambit Declined. Source: https://www.uscfsales.com/media/wysiwyg/page/blog/queens-gambit/queens-gambit-declined-starting-position.jpg

In this variation, Black protects their pawn on d5 with their pawn on c6 instead of accepting the Gambit and falling for the trap. White then attacks Black's d5 pawn with their knight with the move Nc3, and Black again chooses the smart move by playing Nf6, defending the pawn on d5. Right now, the positions are somewhat equal, with control of the center divided between you and your opponent and similar development on both sides. From here on out, whichever color you're playing, you can develop more pieces, protect your king, and go on to win if you use the right tactics.

Overall, the Queen's Gambit is a smart opening that tests both players. So, practice it very well. When you play the Queen's Gambit, you do something really cool: you make a sacrifice. Sacrificing your pieces for more control of the board or for a better position is a move made by elite chess players and Grandmasters.

Quiz

1) Which piece does White move to c4 in the Italian Game opening?

   A) Bishop

   B) Knight

   C) Queen

2) What is Black's first move in the French Defense opening?

   A) Pawn to d5

   B) Pawn to e6

   C) Pawn to c5

3) In the Queen's Gambit opening, which piece does White sacrifice to gain control of the center?

A) Pawn

B) Bishop

C) Queen

Chapter 5: Common Mistakes Made in the Opening and How to Avoid Them

Let's quickly recall what you've learned so far. You've learned the basic principles of chess openings and how they help you on your road to victory. You've learned the value of every piece and seen some examples of positions that change the practical values of chess pieces. After that, you got to know three of the top chess openings worldwide: The Italian Game, the French Defense, and the Queen's Gambit. Right now, you can play any of these three openings and give your opponents a hard time with your moves and tactics.

However, you can't get too confident. Everyone makes mistakes, and mistakes in chess can mean a checkmate. In this chapter, you'll learn about the most common mistakes made in the opening and how to avoid them. The opening phase directly connects to the endgame. If your opening is lacking, your chances of having a good endgame are low. Here are some of the most common opening mistakes made by beginners.

Ignoring the Center

15. Don't ignore the center when playing chess. Source: Conal Gallagher, CC BY 2.0
<https://creativecommons.org/licenses/by/2.0>, via Wikimedia Commons:
https://commons.wikimedia.org/wiki/File:Chess_set_2014.jpg

In every chess game, White's king starts on e1, White's queen starts on d1, Black's king starts on e8, and Black's queen starts on d8. These four pieces are the most valuable and important pieces on any chessboard. The queen is the most powerful weapon you can use to attack your opponent, and your king is the piece you must protect the most, or else you lose the game. The starting squares of the kings and queens are directly connected to the inner center, which consists of the squares e4, e5, d4, and d5. So, if you have control over the center, you have a path to attack your opponent's king right away.

Moreover, the center is where most of the action happens. The rim of the board is not an exciting place to be, whether you're attacking or defending. There's even a famous saying in chess that goes, "A knight on the rim is dim." This is true because a knight is designed to control squares in an elusive way and to attack the opponent from a place they might overlook. During the opening, the rim of the board is the worst place to be unless you're a rook. The best thing to do is attack the center aggressively but with the right pieces at the right time. Recall which pieces to develop first from Chapter 3.

A common thing most beginners do is move too many pawns in the opening. The piece you have the most of is pawns, so it's common not to worry about them. However, they can be as valuable as queens in the right situation. If you move all your pawns at the beginning of the game, many of them will get captured, and you will have a big tactical disadvantage. Moreover, you only have two pawns out of eight that can attack the center, and they need to be defended. If you don't, your opponent will capture them, and that opens you up to attack. Think of pawns as the building blocks of your army. They are the trusty soldiers you can promote to become rooks, bishops, knights, or even queens. This makes them the pieces with the most potential.

Slow Development

Sometimes, you want to take it easy and play slowly and analyze every move carefully, and that is good; however, you must develop your pieces at the right time, or your opponent will have the upper hand. For example, if your opponent has developed both their knights early and you haven't, you are automatically at a disadvantage. Developing your knight early helps you control space and make better moves early on, and it supports your attacking pieces. The same applies to your bishops. Of course, in both cases, you don't have to develop both of your knights or both bishops, but you must control enough space and a decent part of the center to be able to attack your opponent comfortably.

Keep in mind, though, that you must not focus on just developing your knights and bishops. Sometimes, moving your queen early is a good move, even in the opening. If you see a chink in your opponent's armor, capitalize immediately. The goal of the opening is very simple (it's even in the name): to open the game and set yourself up for a good position. A good opening leads to a good middlegame, and a good middlegame leads to a good endgame. If your opening is good enough, you may actually win and make the game shorter.

One more thing you should know about development is when to develop your pawns. Moving them too early makes them vulnerable and robs you of their support in both the middle game and endgame. Focusing your efforts on developing your pawns too early means you don't develop your other pieces early enough. Developing one knight and one pawn is better than developing three pawns. The game situation could dictate something else, but this applies to the general situations. Two pawns and two knights are better than four or five pawns. Keep in mind that this makes it harder for you to castle Kingside and Queenside. If your pawns aren't on the second rank, castling is not a wise move. If you're playing White, your pawns on f2, g2, and h2 should be the last pieces you think about moving, especially if you want your king to be safe.

Too Much Development

You want to develop your pieces, and you want to attack your opponent, and you don't want to lose material (your army of chess pieces as a whole is referred to as a whole, so if you lose a piece, you lose material). To keep it simple, let's use the same example from the first chapter to illustrate this.

You're playing the black pieces. You're strategizing and thinking about tactics as your opponent prepares to make their first move. They start with Nf3. This is called the Zukertort Opening, named after the British-German chess player Johannes Zukertort. You've studied chess openings well, and you're familiar with the principles of this particular opening, so you see that your opponent is now striking at the center from afar. White's knight on f6 controls the e5 and d4 squares.

You decide to play aggressively, and your first move is d5. You have a pawn in the center! Now you've gained some space, and you've opened up some more for your white bishop (starts on c8) to move. Your opponent responds with Ne5. They just pushed their knight right onto the inner center with no defenders. What a confusing move!

Keep calm and remember what you've learned. Your opponent's piece is on its own, so it's not that dangerous. Focus on following the principles. For your second move, you play Nf6. You're now attacking the e4 square with your pawn and your knight. You now have the advantage. Your opponent is scared by the attack and decides to retreat with their knight, playing the move Nd3. You see this great opportunity to attack the center, and you play Nc6. In three moves, you completely control the center with your knights, and you have a pawn in the inner center. Your opponent, on the other hand, has only moved one knight multiple times with no tactical benefit.

It's difficult to experience this scenario in a real game, but the purpose is to show you the cost of moving one piece too much. If you don't move enough pieces, your opponent will give you no chance to breathe and will immediately corner you and have the upper hand. If you want to win and come out of the opening with a good position, you want to develop enough pieces to control a comfortable amount of space but not so much that your defenses are weak. As a general rule, don't move the same piece more than once in the opening.

Neglecting the King

Some players play wonderful openings. They develop the right pieces at the right time, they control the center, and they attack powerfully, yet they forget to protect their king. You have to strike the balance between to find your road to a win. If you focus too much on attacking and you don't defend your king well, you might lose the game early on. If you focus too much on defense and you don't pressure your opponent's king, you simply won't win because all your pieces are behind defending your king and not attacking. The first principle of the opening actually shows you how to do that. If you're playing white and you move your pawn to e4 and your knight to f3, you simultaneously attack the center and defend your pawn. You can apply this to other moves and openings.

Remember that the game is about defending your king and not your other valuable pieces. You must focus all your defense on the king. Castling is your best move when it comes to that. It not only moves your king away from the danger of the center, but it develops one of your rooks. Actually, the rook you develop can be used for sneaky attacks on your opponent's king from far away. If you get a queen in the mix, you may even get a checkmate!

In the piece valuation system you saw in Chapter 2, each piece has a value represented by a number; the pawn's value is 1, the queen's value is 9, etc. There is an extended version of that system that gives the king a value as well, and the king's value in that system in infinity (because if you lose the king, you lose the game). This valuation is funny, but it is true. You must always protect your king.

Undervaluing Your Pieces

Everyone's favorite piece is the queen, right? It's the most powerful, most valuable piece you have in your arsenal. It can attack and control large spaces on the board while being in danger. However, every piece is as important as the next. Some of your pieces are weaker than others, but that doesn't mean you should neglect them. Bishops and knights, while not as strong as the queen, are more valuable pieces than the queen in the opening because of the bishop's versatility and the knight's tricky moves. The queen is not the only piece that can earn you a checkmate, so correctly value your pieces and don't just rely only on it.

Bishops are the snipers of the chessboard. They can control a large number of squares from far away. Consider them your sniper team. They attack and defend from far away. They are very effective in sneak attacks. Knights have their own magical way of moving. They are the only chess pieces that can jump over other pieces, making them hard to catch. Their L-shape movement makes them perfect for double attacks, known as forks, and for controlling influential squares.

Rooks and pawns, while they may not have the queen's flashy moves, they are the backbone of your pieces. Rooks are the only pieces, other than the queen, that can control entire files and ranks on their own, which makes them essential in building strong positions and launching powerful attacks. Pawns, on the other hand, seem weak, but they hold great potential. They are the foot soldiers of your army, slowly advancing and claiming territory on the board. They can create chains where they support each other to form a strong defensive line.

In chess, it's all about teamwork and coordination. Just like any sport, each member of your team has a vital role to play. It's not just about having a powerful queen. It's also about using the unique abilities of every piece and coordinating their moves to achieve victory.

How to Avoid Mistakes in the Opening

You just learned about five of the most common mistakes beginning players make in their chess openings. They are also the most dangerous mistakes because they can give your opponent victory. Now, let's get to the main point of this chapter, which is how to avoid making those mistakes. All you have to do is follow the principles of the opening:

1. Control the center

2. Develop your pieces

3. Protect your king

These three principles are all you need to start your game on the right foot. They give you the best attack and defense opportunities, and they allow you to use all your pieces to their maximum potential. Recall the Italian Game opening from chapter 4, and you can see how these three principles start the 'action' of the game and lead to a decent middle game. The Italian is a prime example of a good opening because it combines all three principles: controlling the center, developing your pieces, and protecting your king.

The French Defense shows you another way to follow the principles of the opening and get an advantage against your opponent, especially if you play with the black pieces. The Queen's Gambit shows you that you don't have to go to the center first. You can set up a better position by moving your pieces in a clever way and tricking your opponent.

Following the rules is great, but you don't always have to stick to them because if you have the same playing style in all of your games, your opponents can easily predict your next move and find their way to a win. Remember that the only rules in chess are how to move your pieces. Your style of play, your opening strategy, your tactics, and every move you make all depend on your choice. That's why you must practice very hard and study as much as you can to become the best chess player you can be. Always challenge yourself and keep studying. That is how you become a better chess player.

Quiz

1) Which of the following moves leads to losing space in the opening phase?

A) Moving one piece more than once

B) Only moving your pawns

C) Developing your queen too early

---

2) True or false: Castling late is the best choice to safeguard your king and move it away from threats.

   A) True

   B) False

3) True or false: Chess is an inflexible game where you must strictly follow the principles of the opening.

   A) True

   B) False

4) Which part of your chess game is more important?

   A) Attacking

   B) Defending

   C) Both are equally important

Chapter 6: Best Ways to Master the Opening Phase in Chess

You've now come to the last chapter of this book. What a fun ride it has been! You've learned about the values of chess pieces, openings, and so much more, and now you have to apply all that knowledge. In this chapter, you'll find some tips and tricks on how to better your chess game and improve your opening so you can have the advantage early on.

Study with Focus

Any chess player who wants to improve and win more games knows they need to study. They have to study everything about the chess game: the opening, the middle game, and the endgame. However, sometimes, you don't know what to start with or what to focus on more. Here's a trick you can use to efficiently divide your time between studying the different phases of a chess game: the 20-40-40 rule.

The 20-40-40 rule says to divide your time between studying the opening, the middlegame, and the endgame with a ratio of 20%, 40%, and 40%, respectively. So, if you're going to study chess for one hundred minutes, study openings for twenty minutes, middlegames for forty minutes, and endgames for forty minutes. This rule can help you bypass the confusion of what to study first, and it's time efficient. You don't have to study for one hundred minutes a day, of course, but you have to dedicate a decent amount of time if you want to get better.

16. The best way to study chess openings is to practice. Source:
https://www.pexels.com/photo/a-boy-playing-chess-6115019/

The best way to study chess openings, and chess in general, is to practice. You can read about openings and watch videos all you want, but this doesn't help you engage with the game. If you study by playing a game, you are guaranteed to improve faster than passively reading books or watching videos. One more thing you can try is taking notes. For example, imagine you're playing with the black pieces, and you decide to play the French Defense. Calmly play your moves and take note of your opponent's moves. Do this for ten consecutive games. Play the same opening and see what your opponent does. Take notes every game and analyze them. You can do this with any opening you like; playing one opening for many consecutive games helps you uncover all its secrets and teaches you how to deal with its different variations and responses.

Focus on Simple Openings

The only rules in chess are how to move the pieces, so you might find an opening with dozens, or even hundreds, of variations. The Italian Game, which is one of the simplest chess openings, has almost infinite continuations. You don't have to study every variation in order to master an opening. All you need is to study the mainline (the most common variation) and know it very well. If you study one with too many variations, you'll end up confused, and you might even forget most of what you're trying to study because of how much time you're spending.

Instead, you should focus on one opening at a time and work on it as hard as you can until you master it. You can try doing one opening a week at first. On the first day of the week, look up the opening and only learn the main variation. Then, on the second day, start playing with it. Follow the main variation and see how your middlegame and endgame go. Then, keep doing this for two days. Now, you can say you know the opening and can play it well. For the next three days of the week, study different variations and have fun with them. For a broader view of the opening, you can analyze a few sample games every day starting from the second day. In this way, you're studying the opening, and you get a peek at how things can go from then on and how you can use different positions to your advantage.

Seeing how it's the simplest one, start with the Italian Game. Study it for a week using the schedule above. Then, take on the French Defense and see how it goes. After that, play the Scandinavian Defense (first move: 1. e4 d5) because it challenges your thinking and allows for versatile play. Later on, you can use the Queen's Gambit because it's a little more advanced than the other ones, and it requires great attacking skills for you to use it to its full potential.

By dedicating your efforts to one opening at a time, you can immerse yourself in its intricacies and practice it extensively until you achieve mastery. Finally, don't be afraid to be creative with an opening as you study it. Change a move, try another approach, do whatever you like. Chess requires intellect and smarts, and a little creativity never hurts. If you're creative with your openings, you might come up with one yourself. Remember that on your road to mastery, you won't become a better player if you keep doing the same thing over and over.

Know Your Plan before Playing

In chess, success isn't just about making moves on the board; it's about thinking ahead of your opponent and outsmarting them. Planning ahead is an essential aspect of chess that sets successful players apart. Before making your first move and kickstarting the action, taking time to plan out your game will make a big difference. Planning in chess takes a few simple steps. First, you have to think ahead. Think about what your opponent can do and what they want to do. This is crucial in the opening phase because your opponent shows you their objective and their playing style. If you play white, you get to start the game as you choose the opening. If you play black, anticipate your opponent's first move and take the game in the direction you want.

After that, consider the possibilities. During the opening phase, you have the most moves to make because most of your pieces are still on the board. Before every move, consider how your opponent might respond and search through the possibilities for the best one you can make that gets you closer to victory. Pay close attention to the whole board because there might be a checkmate hiding somewhere. Do this for your opponent as well. Look for the dangerous moves they can make so you can avoid them and defend better. Also, never hold out hope that your opponent will make a wrong move. Always think they will make the best move.

After you look at the possibilities and consider your moves, plan the game out and draw your road toward victory. Of course, it's almost impossible to plan the entire game out before the first move. However, you can complete your plan after the second or third move, right after you know the opening. When the opening moves have been played, you can easily draw out the rest of the game and carefully walk down the road to victory. Don't be afraid to make a few detours on the way, as some games are unpredictable, after all. If you find the game straying far from the road you planned out for it, guide it back if you can, and if you can't get back to your old road, go with the flow and think your way through. To do this, you have to be flexible in order to adapt to every game you play and be able to use the advantages you have.

Pick the Openings You Like

The only rules in chess are how to move the pieces. Play with the openings you like the most, whether they're the easiest, the simplest, or the ones that match your style. Just like every piece moves in its own special way, every player has their own unique style and personality. Maybe you're a player who likes to focus on the defensive side of the game, maybe you like to play clever moves that surprise your opponent, or maybe you're an aggressive player who attacks right away. In each case, choose an opening that suits your style best.

Here are some tips for choosing your opening. If you're a player who enjoys focusing on defense and waiting for your opponent to make a mistake you can capitalize on, then the French Defense is opening for you. It gives you an early advantage by helping you protect your pieces and allows you to make comfortable moves later in the game. However, if you're an old-fashioned player and you enjoy an authentic style of play, the Italian Game is your best choice. It follows the classic principles of chess, and it's a very popular opening recommended by many chess books. If you're an elusive player who likes to outsmart their opponent and play unexpected moves, your opening is the Queen's Gambit. In the Queen's Gambit, you take control of the center early, and you have an offensive advantage against the opponent.

If you're a calm, cool-headed player who focuses on strategy and playing a patient game, you can play the Ruy Lopez, the Vienna game, or the Sicilian Defense. All of these are sharp openings that lead to strategic battles and offer you a wide range of plans and possibilities. The Sicilian Defense, in particular, adds excitement to your gameplay, making it a great choice if you're a player who enjoys dynamic and exhilarating encounters. The Vienna game strengthens your defense if you're White and allows you to develop your pieces in a strategic fashion.

Finally, remember that the joy of chess isn't just in the outcome. It lies in the whole process. From the first move in the opening to the last move in the endgame, you learn, and you have fun, so enjoy every opening you play, and, again, don't be afraid to mix up your style of play every now and again.

Play Openings with Similar Structures

This part is especially important. When you learn similar chess openings, you have to analyze your games more carefully, and you don't have to make it too complicated. Chess openings are all special, and studying similar ones allows you to appreciate the different qualities of each one. Not only that, but you also learn to keep an eye out for anything unexpected. When you learn similar openings, you must pay close attention to every move and detail in the positions because the slightest difference might lead to a surprising outcome.

Take the Sicilian Defense and the Scandinavian Defense, for example. The Scandinavian Defense starts like this:

1. e4 d5

If White's second move is Nc3, it's called the Scandinavian Defense: Closed variation, while if White's second move is d4, it's called the Blackmar Gambit variation.

Now, the Sicilian Defense:

1. e4 c5

If White follows with Nc3, this is called the Sicilian Defense: Closed variation. If White plays d4, it's called the Smith-Morra Gambit variation.

As you see, the two openings are similar in name and structure, and Black plays an unexpected first move in both. In the Scandinavian, if you're playing White, you don't expect Black to offer you a pawn right away. Games that start with the Scandinavian are mostly tactical and very sharp. If you encounter the Sicilian, you may be surprised that Black is not focusing on the inner center. This seems like an opportunity to take center, but watch out because the Sicilian Defense is popular among both masters and beginners, and this opening can lead to some very exciting games. The challenge here is for you to master both. Study both as best as you can and learn the most popular variations. When you analyze the two together, you'll find some secrets and tweaks that you can make that make the game much more fun and exciting. Here is another example of two similar openings:

The Italian Game goes like this:

1. e4 e5
2. Nf3 Nc6
3. Bc4

The Ruy Lopez opening is played like this:

1. e4 e5
2. Nf3 Nc6
3. Bb5

In the Ruy Lopez, White starts aggressively by attacking Black's knight on c6. This opening usually leads to more aggressive games and a lot of tactical play. The most common move Black plays after White's Bb5 is moving their pawn to a6, attacking the stray bishop. White most commonly retreats one square back, going to a4. The only difference between the Italian and the Ruy Lopez, in the first three moves, is that the bishop moves one extra square. However, this one square makes a big difference later on.

Finally, remember that studying similar chess openings sharpens your analytical skills and fosters adaptability and better strategic thinking, helping you handle unexpected situations with skill and focus. By embracing this challenge, you'll find chess even more fascinating and enjoyable.

Quiz

1) True or False: You should focus on one opening and play it in every single game.

   A) True

   B) False

2) Which of the following pairs of chess openings are similar?

   A) The Scandinavian Defense and the Sicilian Defense

   B) The Ruy Lopez and the French Defense

   C) The Italian Game and the Scandinavian Defense

3) True or False: You should play your chess games on a whim and not plan ahe ad.

   1. True

   2. False

Quiz Answers

Chapter 1

1. B) Controlling the center, developing pieces, and protecting the king

2. A) Moving the same piece twice in a row

3. B) Nc3, attacking the d5 square and protecting the pawn on e4

Chapter 2

1. B) Queen

2. A) Pawn chain

3. A) True

Chapter 3

1. B) Knight to c3 (Nc3)

2. C) Bishop

3. C) Queen

4. D) It influences the mobility and control of the board.

5. A) Pawn to g6

6. C) A famous opening initiated by moving the knight to f3.

7. C) Rook

8. B) The queen's power is unmatched, but it's susceptible to danger.

9. C) Kicking

10. C) Black plays a move that threatens White's queen.

11. D) Controlling the center, developing your pieces, and protecting your king

Chapter 4

1. A) Bishop

2. B) Pawn to e6

3. A) Pawn

Chapter 5

1. A) Moving one piece more than once

2. B) False

3. B) False

4. C) Both are equally important

Chapter 6

1. B) False

2. A) The Scandinavian Defense and the Sicilian Defense

3. B) False

Conclusion

As you reach the end of this chess adventure, stop, and think back on all the things you have learned. Throughout this book, you learned the basic principles of chess openings and how to get a good start in your games. After that, you learned about the values of different chess pieces and discovered how to develop them in the best way possible. Finally, you picked up some helpful tips and tricks for studying chess openings. However, keep in mind that chess is more than just a game. It's a combination of smarts, strategy, and creativity that stood the test of time.

You now have the knowledge and skills necessary to successfully navigate the thrilling challenges that lie beyond the opening: the middlegame and the endgame. The Italian Game, the French Defense, and the Queen's Gambit, the three famous chess openings you've seen in this book, serve as the foundation of mastering chess openings.

But here's a secret: the goal is not to become an expert at openings. The real goal should be to improve as a player, win more games, and, most importantly, have lots of fun playing the game. Learning about openings is like laying a solid foundation for a grand castle or choosing the colors for a brilliant painting. It develops your analytical and problem-solving skills and equips you with the tools you need to take on more difficult chess challenges. Remember that the information you have learned from this book is only the beginning of the wonderful adventure that lies ahead, complete with strategy, tactics, and tough opponents.

Having gained a great knowledge of openings, get ready to enter the middlegame, where imagination soars and tactical choices determine the course of the game. During games, don't be scared to express yourself and experiment with various styles. Chess is an imaginative game, and every move you make gives you a chance to express your special talents and ideas. Never give up when faced with a challenge, even when against a more experienced player. There is always something new to learn.

As your journey with this book ends, remember that the path to mastery is not easy. It takes dedication, practice, and consistency. Every great chess player started as a beginner, overcoming obstacles and setbacks along the way. But with determination and a passion for knowledge, you can conquer any challenge you face. Embrace every game as a chance to improve and learn something new. May this be a helpful resource on your road to becoming a better chess player. Enjoy the process, relish each move, and keep your passion for the game burning.

References

Astle, M. (2022, August 23). The fastest way to learn chess openings. Chessable Blog. https://www.chessable.com/blog/fastest-way-to-learn-openings/

CHESScom, M. F. (2022, September 1). Giuoco Piano. Chess.com. https://www.chess.com/article/view/giuoco-piano-chess-opening

(DanielRensch), D. R. (2018, May 30). The principles of the Opening. Chess.com. https://www.chess.com/article/view/the-principles-of-the-opening

French Defense. (n.d.). Chess.com. https://www.chess.com/openings/French-Defense

Gill. (2023, May 23). Italian game: How to use giuoco piano chess opening. Amphy Blog. https://blog.amphy.com/italian-game-how-to-use-giuoco-piano-chess-opening/

(LuisFSiles), L. F. S. (2019, May 29). The 10 most common chess mistakes among beginners. Chess.com. https://www.chess.com/article/view/the-10-most-common-mistakes-among-chess-beginners

Queen's Gambit - chess openings for kids. (n.d.). Chesskid.com. https://www.chesskid.com/learn/terms/queens-gambit-chess

Scandinavian Defense. (n.d.). Chess.com.
https://www.chess.com/openings/Scandinavian-Defense

Sicilian Defense. (n.d.). Chess.com.
https://www.chess.com/openings/Sicilian-Defense

Similar chess openings? (d4 defenses compared to e4 defenses).
(n.d.). Chess.com. https://www.chess.com/forum/view/chess-
openings/similar-chess-openings-d4-defenses-compared-to-e4-
defenses

Soni, H. (2021a, July 17). The Italian Game. Everything you want
to know about the Italian game. Podium School; Podium
Worksheets and Classes. https://learn.podium.school/chess-
classes/chess-openings-the-italian-game-everything-you-want-to-
know/

Soni, H. (2021b, October 8). The French Defense: A complete
guide to French Defense. Podium School; Podium Worksheets and
Classes. https://learn.podium.school/chess-classes/the-french-
defense-a-complete-guide/

Srikaran. (2021, July 21). Chess Classes for Kids: How to develop
your pieces in chess? Podium School; Podium Worksheets and
Classes. https://learn.podium.school/chess-classes/how-to-
develop-your-pieces-in-chess/

Vienna Game. (n.d.). Chess.com.
https://www.chess.com/openings/Vienna-Game

Made in United States
Troutdale, OR
11/02/2024

24365531R00050